MACRO ECONOMICS

CANADA IN THE GLOBAL ENVIRONMENT

FIFTH EDITION

MICHAEL PARKIN
University of Western Ontario

ROBIN BADE

PEARSON

Addison
Wesley

Toronto

Vice President, Editorial Director:	Michael J. Young
Acquisitions Editor:	Gary Bennett
Marketing Manager:	Deborah Meredith
Senior Developmental Editor:	Suzanne Schaan
Senior Production Editor:	Marisa D'Andrea
Copy Editor:	Laurel Sparrow
Production Coordinator:	Deborah Starks
Permissions and Photo Research:	Lisa Brant
Page Layout:	Bill Renaud
Illustrator:	Richard Parkin
Art Director:	Mary Opper
Interior and Cover Design:	Anthony Leung
Cover Image (background):	Gary Holscher/Gettyimages
Cover Image (spot image):	Michael Pohuski/Gettyimages

National Library of Canada Cataloguing in Publication

Parkin, Michael, 1939–
    Macroeconomics : Canada in the global environment / Michael Parkin,
    Robin Bade — 5th ed.

Includes index.
ISBN 0-321-15412-6

1. Macroeconomics.   2. Canada—Economic conditions—1991–
I. Bade, Robin   II. Title.

HB172.5.P363 2003   339   C2002-902847-7

Statistics Canada information is used with the permission of the Minister of
Industry, as Minister responsible for Statistics Canada. Information on the
availability of the wide range of data from Statistics Canada can be obtained
from Statistics Canada's Regional Offices, its World Wide Web site at
http://www.statcan.ca, and its toll-free access number 1-800-263-1136.

PEARSON

Addison
Wesley

ABOUT THE AUTHORS

MICHAEL PARKIN received his training as an economist at the Universities of Leicester and Essex in England. Currently in the Department of Economics at the University of Western Ontario, Canada, Professor Parkin has held faculty appointments at Brown University, the University of Manchester, the University of Essex, and Bond University. He is a past president of the Canadian Economics Association and has served on the editorial boards of the *American Economic Review* and the *Journal of Monetary Economics* and as managing editor of the *Canadian Journal of Economics*. Professor Parkin's research on macroeconomics, monetary economics, and international economics has resulted in over 160 publications in journals and edited volumes, including the *American Economic Review*, the *Journal of Political Economy*, the *Review of Economic Studies*, the *Journal of Monetary Economics*, and the *Journal of Money, Credit and Banking*. He became most visible to the public with his work on inflation that discredited the use of wage and price controls. Michael Parkin also spearheaded the movement toward European monetary union.

ROBIN BADE earned degrees in mathematics and economics at the University of Queensland and her Ph.D. at the Australian National University. She has held faculty appointments in the business schools at the University of Edinburgh and Bond University and in the economics departments at the University of Manitoba, the University of Toronto, and the University of Western Ontario. Her research on international capital flows appears in the *International Economic Review* and the *Economic Record*.

Professor Parkin and Dr. Bade are the joint authors of *Modern Macroeconomics* (Pearson Education Canada), an intermediate text, and *Foundations of Economics* (Pearson Education Canada), and have collaborated on many research and textbook writing projects. They are both experienced and dedicated teachers of introductory economics.